Love Feast

How Pastoral Care can be practiced by all, and how the care of souls can invite all to God's table

An interactive curriculum for individuals, small groups and congregations seeking to share God's love

Love Feast is a curriculum designed to equip and educate an individual, an entire congregation, or a specified group of individuals, for pastoral care actions within a church or a community. Its roots are founded in a class at Memphis Theological Seminary called Introduction to the Theology and Practice of Pastoral Care taught by Dr. Lee Ramsey.

About the writer: Dusty Luthy is a youth min-ister and part-time librarian based in Paducah, Ky. She is pursuing her Master of Divinity de-gree at Memphis Theological Seminary. Dusty has a Bachelor's degree in Journalism from the University of Missouri, and spent six years as a sports writer before answering God's call to ministry.

Published by the Discipleship Ministry Team of the Ministry Council, Cumberland Presbyterian Church. 8207 Traditional Place, Cordova, Tennessee, 38016.

ISBN:978-1-945929-17-5

Copyright 2018

Table of Contents

2	Welcome & Introduction
4	Supplies & Topics
8	Appetizers
12	Main Course
25	Side Dish – Grief & Loss
28	Side Dish – Divorce
31	Side Dish – Physical & Mental Illness
34	Side Dish – Addiction
38	Side Dish – Veterans & PTSD
41	Dessert – Worship
44	Personal Reflection
45	Bibliography

Why the pineapple?

The pineapple, once a rarity found in kitchens and on tables around the world, is a European symbol of hospitality. When a pineapple was found as decoration at a meal or home, a guest would know he or she was welcome into that household and the host or hostess would be a generous and loving one.

May we all strive to be beacons of hospitality, welcome, love, and generosity in a world that needs the Light.

Welcome and Introduction

Why a Love Feast? So much of Jesus' life and ministry centered around meals. He turned water into wine at a wedding reception. Jesus and his disciples fed 5,000 people through the modest offerings of fish and bread. He ate with tax collectors and sinners, one of the Pharisee's biggest reasons for wanting to annihilate him. Jesus dined with his disciples the night he was betrayed and arrested, sharing the bread and the wine as symbols for his impending sacrifice of body and blood.

And of course, upon his resurrection, he appeared to his disciples and said, "Hey! What's for dinner?" His disciples gave him a piece of broiled fish, and he ate it in front of them (Luke 24:41-43).

Historically, the Love Feast was a fellowship meal in which ancient Christians engaged. It is intimate to share a meal with someone; to break bread with another is one of the most sincere forms of love and friendship and fellowship we still have 2,000 years after Jesus' death.

Some want us to build higher walls. I join with other voices and say, let's build a longer table.

"Therefore welcome one another as Christ has welcomed you, for the glory of God." (Romans 15:7, ESV)

But in order to extend the invitation to the table, we must make sure everyone feels welcome, and that they are assured of Christ's love, care, sustaining, guiding, healing, and restoration.

Which means you and I have a lot of work to do.

The Love Feast curriculum is organized.... well, according to a fine dining meal experience. It can be consumed all in one day as a workshop, or in smaller portions and sessions as your needs dictate. It can also be consumed individually.

* There are Appetizers which are ice breakers, activities and questions to warm up your audience and prepare them for what is to come. If you are going solo, use these prompts as journal entries.

* There's the Main Course — sometimes referred to as "meat and potatoes" if you're from the country like I am. This is scriptural, traditional, and historic framework to give us a basis for our endeavors into Pastoral Care.

* Side Dishes are items that can be ordered a la cart, or put on the table for a full feast. These include forays into specific issues of pastoral care and needs of individuals within a congregation or community such as divorce, depression, illness, death, PTSD, etc. You can discuss all of these issues at your own pace, or pick and choose what is close to your heart, your call and the Spirit's direction!

* Dessert is the joyous time of a meal, and for us as Christians, that means worship. Take these ideas to worship together as a way to wind down from the program. At its most basic form, this is a time to share Holy Communion with one another — the ultimate symbol of a Love Feast we have today.

* Every good meal has a time of Reflection. This is when you internalize and process what has just been served to you and consumed. Spend this time in prayer, meditation, journaling, discussion or quiet thought.

Blessings as you seek to serve and care for God's creation.

In Christ,
~ Dusty

Curriculum Topics

The Workshop Topics of Addiction, Veterans & PTSD, Divorce, Death & Loss, and Physical & Mental Illness were chosen over other equally worthy crisis-related topics based on the commonalities of such things found in congregations and communities in any location, size or context. Should your congregation find itself ministering to a large number of young parents, consider creating your own workshop topic on Child Rearing & Parenting and switching another out. Perhaps your church cares for the homeless population — certainly tailor the curriculum and program to best fit the needs of your church.

This curriculum has been designed to give you an introduction to each issue. It is by no means a definitive authority or source on such events. To add to your program or event, consider these tips:

■ Invite a local expert to speak on one of the chosen topics. Example: A Christian divorce counselor will certainly have great insights for ministering to divorcees. The local health department, seminary, community college, university or even a public library can help you find an authoritative voice.

■ Ask someone in your congregation or community with a solid testimony to consider sharing their story of how the Church, acting as the hands and feet of Jesus Christ, reached out to minister to him or her during a time of crisis.

■ Take a field trip. Get out of the church. Schedule a tour to an addiction counseling facility, VA hospital or even a funeral home. Ask those who minister and help those people first-hand how you can better love and care for others.

Supplies:
- Pens/pencils
- Paper/journals
- Individual candies such as M&Ms, mints, etc.
- Large writing space such as white board or newsprint
- FOOD
- Extra resources from local agencies (optional)

Sample Schedules

Love Feast 5

Use these sample schedules to create your own workshop day or series of sessions. Consider a Saturday, or even a Sunday right after morning worship concludes. Personalize the event or change the schedule however best fits your audience!

Workshop format

Not too early!

10 a.m.	Registration
10:30 a.m.	Welcome and announcements
10:45 a.m.	Appetizers
11:45 a.m.	Break
Noon	Lunch
12:45 p.m.	Main Course
1:30 p.m.	Break
1:40 p.m.	Side Dish 1
2:10 p.m.	Side Dish 2
2:40 p.m.	Side Dish 3
3:10 p.m.	Side Dish 4
3:40 p.m.	Break
4:00 p.m.	Dessert
4:40 p.m.	Reflection
5 p.m.	Dismiss

Consider a potluck!!

Allow participants to pick 4 sessions out of 5 provided to attend in breakout sessions led by other leaders in the church or outside professionals; add a half hour to the schedule if you want to hit all 5

Communion and Worship

Session format

Week 1: Introduction (10 minutes), Appetizers (45 minutes), Main Course Part 1 (30 minutes) = Total: 1 hour 25 minutes

Week 2: Welcome (10 minutes), Appetizer (10 minutes), Main Course Part 2 (30 minutes), Reflection (15 minutes) = Total: 1 hour 5 minutes

Week 3: Welcome (10 minutes), Side Dish 1 (25 minutes), Side Dish 2 (25 minutes), Dessert (20 minutes) = Total: 1 hour 20 minutes

Week 4: Welcome (10 minutes), Side Dish 3 (25 Minutes), Side Dish 4 (25 minutes), Dessert (20 minutes) = Total: 1 hour 20 minutes

Week 5: Welcome (10 minutes), Side Dish 5 (25 minutes), Dessert (20 minutes), Reflection (20 minutes) = Total: 1 hour 15 minutes

Week 6: Welcome (10 minutes), Love Feast! (as time allows), Dessert (10 minutes), Reflection (20 minutes) = Total: ??

Love Feast: Appetizers

Use these appetizers as a way to whet the appetite — make participants more comfortable and familiar with each other and the topic of pastoral care. Feel free to use all of the activities, pick only a couple that you like, or add your own. If you're consuming this feast of a curriculum on your own, use these prompts as journal entries.

Appetizer 1

Instruct each member to take a handful of candies (such as M&Ms, Skittles, mints, etc.) — more than 2 and fewer than 10. Without eating them, have each participant name a favorite food aloud for each candy represented. If I had 4 candies, I would say Double Stuf Oreos, French fries, homegrown tomatoes, and sugar snap peas. If your group is large, break up into smaller groups of 4-5. Be sure to include introductions if your group isn't familiar with one another. After you share, eat the candies!

Discussion Question: What's the most important factor in preparing a feast? Who should be invited? Does a particular meal you've shared with others stand out as memorable to you?

Love Feast: Appetizers

Appetizer 2

Partner up, look at your partner, and repeat together: God loves you….and I'm trying.

Yeah, it's OK to laugh!

Together read this scripture from Matthew 22:36-40:

36 "'Teacher, which is the great commandment in the Law?' 37 And he said to him, 'You shall love the Lord your God with all your heart and with all your soul and with all your mind. 38 This is the great and first commandment. 39 And a second is like it: You shall love your neighbor as yourself. 40 On these two commandments depend all the Law and the Prophets.'" Matthew 22:36-40 ESV

Discussion Question: Is it harder to love God, or to love others? Why do you stand by your response?

Love God. Love your neighbor. How successful are Christians at following these seemingly simple rules?

Love Feast: Appetizers

Appetizer 3

What is Pastoral Care? On a white board, chalk board, newsprint or individual sheets of paper, create a bubble map. In the center, write "Pastoral Care" and circle it. As you come up with ideas, examples, and definitions of Pastoral Care, write them around the center bubble, circle them, and connect the bubbles to the center with a straight line. This visual mapping can help organize your thoughts as we process Pastoral Care.

Discussion Question: What makes Pastoral Care different than being a good neighbor or a good friend?

Love Feast: Appetizers

Appetizer 4

How have you seen Pastoral Care enacted in your congregation in the past? Make a list of actions taken by individuals or the church as a whole that exemplify Pastoral Care.

How have you personally received Pastoral Care from those in your congregation or pastor? Make a list of those actions, as well.

Discussion Question: Who is qualified to give Pastoral Care? How can one become qualified?

Love Feast: Appetizers

Appetizer 5

Case study

Monte Campbell and his family just moved from the bustling metropolis of Hanover City to the tiny town of Maysprings. He and his wife, BethAnn, and two sons, Roger and Roy, have been coming to your church for several Sundays now.

You have found out a few things about the Campbell family through the Sunday School Grapevine: Monte is an Iraq war veteran with a few lingering battle injuries, and is currently unemployed. BethAnn works as a paralegal at a small law firm. Roger and Roy are BethAnn's biological sons from a previous marriage.

You and your church could respond and minister to this new family in several ways.

Discuss which of the following response(s) would be the most appropriate and successful given your congregation, resources, idea of pastoral care, ministry goals and theology — and which one(s) might be the most likely to actually happen. Discuss how some of these responses may be flawed in their approach.

If your group is large, divide up into smaller groups of 3-4.

✔ **Option 1:**
Do nothing. Your church is fun, vibrant, theologically sound, and dagnabbit, people like you! The Campbells will join the church, or they won't. It's their call, not yours.

✔ **Option 2:**
Invite them personally to the upcoming church Fall Festival. Have your fellow Sunday School members extend personal invitations, too. Be sure and introduce Roger and Roy to the Youth Group leader. Say a prayer that the family shows up. It's in God's hands, now.

✔ **Option 3:**
Report your findings to the lead pastor of your church. After all, this is what you pay her for, and it is her job to court and woo new members to your church.

✔ **Option 4:**
Catch the Campbells in the parking lot. Introduce yourself and your family. Invite them over for lunch or out to eat. At the end of the meal, exchange cell phone numbers and addresses. Later that evening, you text the family to let them know they are in your prayers and to say how much you enjoyed lunch. You connect with the family via social media, and make plans for another outing.

Love Feast: Appetizers

✔ **Option 5:**
Let the Campbell family know they've been sitting in your pew, the same pew your family has occupied now for three generations, and they need to find a new place to sit if they're going to keep attending Sunday morning worship.

✔ **Option 6:**
You open up a dialogue with Monte by thanking him for his service in Iraq. You ask how he and his wife and family have adjusted to the move from the big city to the smaller town. He responds that it's been hard for everyone in his family to make friends in a town where everybody already knows one another. After discussing the issue with your spouse and Bible Study group, you decide to host a backyard cookout for the Campbells, being sure to invite families of similar nuclear makeup to mingle and mix.

✔ **Option 7:**
You introduce the family to Robert. Robert is your congregation's go-to guy. Robert knows everyone, and everyone knows Robert. If you want something done in this town, you start with Robert. Robert instantly befriends Monte, and sets about finding him a fulfilling job. You invite Beth-Ann out for coffee, and volunteer your teenage daughter to babysit Roger and Roy. You and BethAnn have a lot in common, and you invite her to your weekly Bible Study.

✔ **Option 8:**
Avoid the Campbells. You didn't agree with the war then, and you still don't now. Plus, those guys who went overseas are coming back with severe PTSD. You certainly don't want him blowing up your church or your family. You secretly hope they don't come back.

✔ **Option 9:**
Grab your significant other and introduce yourselves to the family. Ask how they like the worship sessions so far. Ask specifically how you and your spouse can pray for the family. Ask how the church can best serve them as they transition to this new city.

✔ **Option 10:**
You can already tell you won't have anything in common with this new family, so you corner and convince your best friend's two children to invite Roy and Roger over to play. You promise the children $5 each if they can get Roy and Roger to accept the invitation.

Love Feast: Main Course

Use what follows as the framework and foundation for your introduciton to Pastoral Care. This portion of the Feast should answer the **Who, What, When, Where, and Why** questions.

What is Pastoral Care:

Pastoral Care is a continuation of Jesus Christ's own ministry of care through the church and its representatives in the world. Pastoral Care refers to the caring concern of the church towards persons, families, groups, and communities in times of joy or in times of trouble or distress (Ramsey).

Care of Souls

Care of Souls is a traditional term for Pastoral Care. It's Latin roots includes the term "cure," so sometimes "cure of souls" is repeated. The term "Care of Souls" is used three ways:

    1. Care of Souls sums up the actions of a lead clergy member, acknowledging that all acts of ministry have as their ultimate aim the salvation and perfection of persons under God.

    2. Care of Souls can also be used in a narrower context, known as *seelsorge* (soul care), which was promoted by Martin Luther during the Protestant Reformation.

    3. Care of Souls can simply be a synonym for Pastoral Care. The Concise Dictionary of Pastoral Care and Counseling repeats W.A. Clebsch and C.R. Jaekle's 1975 definition of Care of Souls as thus: **"helping acts done by representative Christian persons directed toward the healing, sustaining, guiding, and reconciling of troubled persons whose troubles arise in the context of ultimate meanings and concerns"** (Asquith 8).

4 Goals of Pastoral Care:

- Healing
- Guiding
- Sustaining
- Reconciling

Love Feast: Main Course

For care to be "pastoral" it may refer either to the office of the religious leader or to the motivation/attitude/characterizing of the caregiver (Asquith 51).

Who can DO Pastoral Care?

- ✔ Pastor or priest
- ✔ Elder or deacon
- ✔ Youth Minister
- ✔ Organist
- ✔ Children
- ✔ Associate minister
- ✔ Church member
- ✔ Acolyte
- ✔ Church secretary
- ✔ Anyone!

■ **Ordained or acknowledged leader**

Shares: resources, wisdom, expertise to act as authority of the religious community.

■ **Member of Religious Community**

Has same: values, commitments, motivation as the rest of the group.

(Asquith 51)

ANYONE can be used to effectively minister to another person, group, community or church.

When does someone NEED Pastoral Care?

■ **Times of Crisis:** death, loss, mental illness, physical illness, trauma, abuse, addiction, neglect, divorce, war, etc.

■ **Times of Joy:** marriage, birth, promotion, spiritual growth, reunion, anniversaries, etc.

Love Feast: Main Course

Who RECEIVES Pastoral Care?

- ✔ Individual
- ✔ Community
- ✔ Nation
- ✔ Family
- ✔ Church
- ✔ World

How might Pastoral Care **be received by** each of these categories? Give specific examples if you can.

Individual:

Family:

Church:

Community:

Nation:

World:

Love Feast: Main Course

How might Pastoral Care look differently **coming from** those in this list?

Clergy:

Lay member:

Small Group:

Congregation:

Because of sin, caring for others pastorally is not always a natural thing to do. It's why loving our neighbor can be harder than loving God. (See Appetizer 2)

Take this time to list reasons which may prevent you from naturally engaging in Pastoral Care.

Love Feast: Main Course

Now that we understand what Pastoral Care looks like, and who can engage in it, where does Pastoral Care come from?

Caring Traditions in **Scripture** (Ramsey)

As you read this scripture silently or out loud in a group, highlight or underline words or phrases that stand out to you. Consider engaging one or all of these texts in a *lectio divina* method — reading over the scripture silently and out loud numerous times, prayerfully meditating on the scripture, asking the Holy Spirit to reveal to you a new way of understanding an old text.

1. Pastor as **shepherd** of the faithful community, tending to the needs of the members and building up the people of God:

Ephesians 4:11-12
"11 And he gave the apostles, the prophets, the evangelists, the shepherds and teachers, 12 to equip the saints for the work of ministry, for building up the body of Christ." Ephesians 4:11-12 ESV

1 Peter 5:1-4
"So I exhort the elders among you, as a fellow elder and a witness of the sufferings of Christ, as well as a partaker in the glory that is going to be revealed: 2 shepherd the flock of God that is among you, exercising oversight, not under compulsion, but willingly, as God would have you; not for shameful gain, but eagerly; 3 not domineering over those in your charge, but being examples to the flock. 4 And when the chief Shepherd appears, you will receive the unfading crown of glory." 1 Peter 5:1-4 ESV

Ezekiel 34:
"The word of the Lord came to me: 2 'Son of man, prophesy against the shepherds of Israel; prophesy, and say to them, even to the shepherds, Thus says the Lord God: Ah, shepherds of Israel who have been feeding yourselves! Should not shepherds feed the sheep? 3 You eat the fat, you clothe yourselves with the wool, you slaughter the fat ones, but you do not feed the sheep. 4 The weak you have not strengthened, the sick you have not healed, the in-

Love Feast: Main Course

jured you have not bound up, the strayed you have not brought back, the lost you have not sought, and with force and harshness you have ruled them. 5 So they were scattered, because there was no shepherd, and they became food for all the wild beasts. My sheep were scattered; 6 they wandered over all the mountains and on every high hill. My sheep were scattered over all the face of the earth, with none to search or seek for them.

7 'Therefore, you shepherds, hear the word of the Lord: 8 As I live, declares the Lord God, surely because my sheep have become a prey, and my sheep have become food for all the wild beasts, since there was no shepherd, and because my shepherds have not searched for my sheep, but the shepherds have fed themselves, and have not fed my sheep, 9 therefore, you shepherds, hear the word of the Lord: 10 Thus says the Lord God, Behold, I am against the shepherds, and I will require my sheep at their hand and put a stop to their feeding the sheep. No longer shall the shepherds feed themselves. I will rescue my sheep from their mouths, that they may not be food for them.
11 'For thus says the Lord God: Behold, I, I myself will search for my sheep and will seek them out. 12 As a shepherd seeks out his flock when he is among his sheep that have been scattered, so will I seek out my sheep, and I will rescue them from all places where they have been scattered on a day of clouds and thick darkness. 13 And I will bring them out from the peoples and gather them from the countries, and will bring them into their own land. And I will feed them on the mountains of Israel, by the ravines, and in all the inhabited places of the country. 14 I will feed them with good pasture, and on the mountain heights of Israel shall be their grazing land. There they shall lie down in good grazing land, and on rich pasture they shall feed on the mountains of Israel. 15 I myself will be the shepherd of my sheep, and I myself will make them lie down, declares the Lord God. 16 I will seek the lost, and I will bring back the strayed, and I will bind up the injured, and I will strengthen the weak, and the fat and the strong I will destroy. I will feed them in justice.

17 'As for you, my flock, thus says the Lord God: Behold, I judge between sheep and sheep, between rams and male goats. 18 Is it not enough for you to feed on the good pasture, that you must tread down with your feet the rest of your pasture; and to drink

Love Feast: Main Course

of clear water, that you must muddy the rest of the water with your feet? 19 And must my sheep eat what you have trodden with your feet, and drink what you have muddied with your feet?

20 'Therefore, thus says the Lord God to them: Behold, I, I myself will judge between the fat sheep and the lean sheep. 21 Because you push with side and shoulder, and thrust at all the weak with your horns, till you have scattered them abroad, 22 I will rescue my flock; they shall no longer be a prey. And I will judge between sheep and sheep. 23 And I will set up over them one shepherd, my servant David, and he shall feed them: he shall feed them and be their shepherd. 24 And I, the Lord, will be their God, and my servant David shall be prince among them. I am the Lord; I have spoken.

25 'I will make with them a covenant of peace and banish wild beasts from the land, so that they may dwell securely in the wilderness and sleep in the woods. 26 And I will make them and the places all around my hill a blessing, and I will send down the showers in their season; they shall be showers of blessing. 27 And the trees of the field shall yield their fruit, and the earth shall yield its increase, and they shall be secure in their land. And they shall know that I am the Lord, when I break the bars of their yoke, and deliver them from the hand of those who enslaved them. 28 They shall no more be a prey to the nations, nor shall the beasts of the land devour them. They shall dwell securely, and none shall make them afraid. 29 And I will provide for them renowned plantations so that they shall no more be consumed with hunger in the land, and no longer suffer the reproach of the nations. 30 And they shall know that I am the Lord their God with them, and that they, the house of Israel, are my people, declares the Lord God. 31 And you are my sheep, human sheep of my pasture, and I am your God, declares the Lord God.'"
Ezekiel 34:1-31 ESV

2. Pastor as priest, who intercedes (like Christ) with God on our behalf

Hebrews 4:14-16
"14 Since then we have a great high priest who has passed through the heavens, Jesus, the Son of God, let us hold fast our confes-

Love Feast: Main Course

sion. 15 For we do not have a high priest who is unable to sympathize with our weaknesses, but one who in every respect has been tempted as we are, yet without sin. 16 Let us then with confidence draw near to the throne of grace, that we may receive mercy and find grace to help in time of need." Hebrews 4:14-16 ESV

3. Congregation as the <u>priesthood</u> of all believers…

1 Peter 2:9
"9 But you are a chosen race, a royal priesthood, a holy nation, a people for his own possession, that you may proclaim the excellencies of him who called you out of darkness into his marvelous light." 1 Peter 2:9 ESV

4. … who <u>bear</u> one another's burdens and <u>teach</u> one another in all wisdom

Colossians 3:12-17
"12 Put on then, as God's chosen ones, holy and beloved, compassionate hearts, kindness, humility, meekness, and patience, 13 bearing with one another and, if one has a complaint against another, forgiving each other; as the Lord has forgiven you, so you also must forgive. 14 And above all these put on love, which binds everything together in perfect harmony. 15 And let the peace of Christ rule in your hearts, to which indeed you were called in one body. And be thankful. 16 Let the word of Christ dwell in you richly, teaching and admonishing one another in all wisdom, singing psalms and hymns and spiritual songs, with thankfulness in your hearts to God. 17 And whatever you do, in word or deed, do everything in the name of the Lord Jesus, giving thanks to God the Father through him." Colossians 3:12-17

Love Feast: Main Course

Caring Leaders in Hebrew Scripture

■ **Prophets** - Care for the religious tradition and faithfulness to God's ways
■ **Priests** - Care for the worship and ritual life of God's community
■ **Wisdom leaders (teachers, counselors)** - care for individuals and families through guidance and wise counsel (Ramsey)

What characters in the Old Testament can you list who would be considered shepherds of God's people?

Give specific examples of their care for God's people and those around them.

Love Feast: Main Course

Caring Leaders in the Church

When pastor is used in the New Testament, it tends to mean "shepherd" when translated from its Greek origins.

What are the characteristics associated with a shepherd?

How does a pastor (or priest or other clergy member) act like a shepherd to his or her congregation?

How might you act like a shepherd to those around you? List concrete examples.

Love Feast: Main Course

History of Pastoral Care in the Early Church (Ramsey)

Why should the 21st century Church study history? For us, it's important to read the Bible in its context to understand its true meaning, and sometimes finding historical background is the only way to do this. It's also important for the Church to examine its past to better understand how to evaluate its work and mission in the present, and it's movement in the future.

Early Church - Jesus Christ to 180 CE
Pastoral Care is seen as sustaining the believer as he or she awaits the return of Christ in an often hostile world

Four Modes of sustaining in Pastoral Care in the Early Church:

    1. **Preservation** - Pastor holds the line against further loss or alienation (emotional, physical, spiritual)

    2. **Consolation** - Pastor offers timely consolation (words, actions, suggestions and solutions) to connect those who are suffering to the community of hope (easy to jump to this before preservation)

    3. **Consolidation** - Pastor assists the broken to begin picking up the pieces of their lives and begin to live anew

    4. **Redemption** - Pastor sustains the believer by helping him or her discover something truly redemptive out of the suffering undergone.

When might Pastoral Care such as the four modes listed above be offered in our present churches? Are these modes of ancient Pastoral Care so different than what is offered in the present day?

Love Feast: Main Course

Protestant Reformation (Ramsey)

Reformation 1350-1600

1. Pastoral Care focused upon the individual's **relationship** with God — parishioner can go directly to God with no need for an intermediary like a priest
2. Pastoral Care as <u>reconciliation</u> — pastors developed the art of helping believers become reconciled to God and neighbor. This was done through careful pastoral discipline of the believer.
3. Pastors held believers **accountable** to God and the community for the sake of reconciliation
4. Rise of **small groups** for spiritual care (Pietistic tradition)

Martin Luther (1483-1546) — an Augustinian monk and one of the most well-known leaders of the Reformation, challenged the corruption in the Catholic church, and called for extensive reform

One of Luther's lasting contributions to ministry was his view of pastoral leadership. Luther advocated using the word pastor instead of priest as the title of a church's leader — this would be indicative of how that leader is viewed by that congregation.

Priest vs. Pastor = Historic Definitions

Priest: bridge between humanity and God; an intermediary

Pastor: leads, guides, directs humanity to reconciliation and direct relationship with God

Luther focused on the priesthood of **all** believers, or the **pastorhood of all believers**. God's Word is not reserved for clergy. As baptized Christians, we are all called into ministry and conversation with God.

Love Feast: Main Course

Traditional Pastoral Care

What are the Pastoral Care traditions of your tradition, denomination or congregation? Does your church place an emphasis on the Eucharist as a sacrament? Is prayer a focus?

Take this time to share and talk about what ministering to others looks like in your context. Consider listing ministries of care of your congregation or ones you've been a part of in your community.

Side Dish: Grief and Loss

Grief and Loss

Death is most likely the crisis of which a church is most used to offering Pastoral Care. Funerals are part of the church culture, and no one can escape death this side of heaven. Grief is an emotion or state of being felt after experiencing a loss, including death. However, individuals can experience grief for various types of loss.

Two categories of Loss: (Ramsey)

Physical (tangible) — a beloved person, toy, book, car, pet
Symbolic (psycho-social) — a role, a dream, divorce

Looking at Loss More Specifically: (Ramsey)

- Material loss — loss of a thing or an object, such as a family heirloom, house, car, etc.

- Relationship loss — breakups, death, divorce — a change in status of a relationship

- Intra-psychic loss — dreams, hopes, ideals, perhaps memory loss, PTSD

- Functional loss — physical impediments such as infirmity, continence, walking, sight, hearing, sound (can be normal and predictable)

- Role loss — loss of a life purpose, such as retirement, divorce, job loss, an identity shift

- Systemic loss — school systems, corporations, churches

Change, even when it's progress, can be shattering and cause grief.

Side Dish: Grief and Loss

Grief is a process with identifiable stages or phases during which an individual

- gives up that which is lost.
- withdraws emotional investment in the physical reality of the other.
- effects gradual reinvestment of one's self in the images of the other that are part of the self.
- renews meaningful activities and relationships without the lost one.

All of these stages must be gone through at the person's own pace in order for positive reorganization to take place. (Asquith 202)

Stages of Grief
made popular by Elizabeth Kubler-Ross

1. Shock
2. Denial
3. Anger
4. Bargaining
5. Acceptance

There is no timeline for processing grief or loss. An individual who has experienced a loss may go through several phases of healing numerous times.

Things NOT to say to a grieving individual:

✗ You're still young enough to get married again.
✗ God needed her more than we did.
✗ He's in a better place.
✗ How are you doing?
✗ *Nothing*
✗ God is in control.
✗ You can still have other children.
✗ God never gives us more than we can handle.

Side Dish: Grief and Loss

Grief can look different according to timing of loss (Ramsey)

- *Sudden or traumatic loss* — unanticipated loss, such as car accident or suicide, that causes profound shock. Bereaved can respond with denial or heroic response. This type of grief can isolate survivors.

- *Anticipatory grief* — the dying person AND family and friends must grieve before the final loss. The dying person will lose all they've ever known; the family/friends will lose one person. Sometimes easier to process than sudden loss.

- *Chronic sorrow* — when grief comes with "no end" such as in cases of Alzheimer's, stroke victims, imprisonment, birth defects, or chronic, severe illnesses. Can be corrosive of ongoing relationships.

- *Near Miss Grief* — survivor's guilt. Not common, but hidden from outward observation.

- *Tragic Sense of Life* — second-hand grief, occurs among those who spend a lot of time around others who grieve or are caught in tragic circumstances. "Helping" professions are those who most often experience this form of grief.

- *Pathological grief* — when an individual becomes stuck in grief and sadness, becomes morbid, sick or atypical and includes symptoms such as depression, anxiety, addictions, lack of social interaction. Professional help is needed.

Platitudes are never comforting. Instead, offer real, heartfelt grief and support.

Be cautious if you've been "there" before…a person in grief fresh after a loss may not be ready to hear truths about grief, moving forward, or otherwise.

Side Dish: Divorce

Divorce

Individuals who are separated, divorcing, or have been divorced are prevalent throughout churches, but are often an invisible population of people amidst your pews. Divorce is one of life's current crises that the Bible actually speaks of, and often quite negatively. Regardless of the reasons behind divorce, consider ministering attentively to this hurting group of people.

Divorce Statistics

Marriage rate: 6.9 per 1,000
Divorce rate: 3.2 per 1,000
(https://www.cdc.gov/nchs/fastats/marriage-divorce.htm)

The American Psychology Association says that 90 percent of people in Western cultures get married by the age of 50, and the divorce rate is still active at 40 to 50 percent, although it's likely closer to 40. The rate increases for those in subsequent marriages.
(http://www.apa.org/topics/divorce/)

Who is getting a divorce?
An article from *Psychology Today* suggests:

- Baby Boomers have a high divorce rate
- People with higher incomes and more education seek divorces less frequently
- Those without a college degree also tend to divorce at higher rates

(https://www.psychologytoday.com/blog/living-single/201702/what-is-the-divorce-rate-really)

While divorce is certainly a form of loss, unique to divorce is the feeling of <u>rejection</u> and <u>failure</u> felt by an individual.

Side Dish: Divorce

Divorce has been termed "a death, only without a burial." There is serious grief involved in a divorce, as well as the gamut of other feelings. Individuals can experience fear of the future without their significant other, guilt for their role in the separation, anger at the experience, relief at being out of a bad situation, joy at being liberated, numbness at the pain, etc.

For individuals in the church, divorce carries a stigma unlike other forms of loss or crisis. Scripture, tradition and history often tell us that divorce isn't to be condoned, accepted or tolerated. Divorced individuals report being ostracized by more conservative churches, even if the divorce was due to abuse, infidelity or addiction.

Discuss your denomination or tradition's view on divorce. How has the church treated individuals who are divorced?

If churches are more open about divorcees, many focus on saving troubled marriages, or preventing divorce at all costs. Very few minister to divorcees AFTER the divorce.

Brainstorm some ways you and your church can be more welcoming to divorcees. What are some ways you and your church can care for these individuals?

Still interested in helping others heal from divorce? Visit the Divorce Care website (https://www.divorcecare.org) and learn how to start a group at your church, or visit one in action in your community.

Side Dish: Divorce

More practical ideas for ministering to divorcees:

✔ Don't say, "Let me know if I can help in any way." Pride, or even shame, will often keep a divorcee (or anyone going through tragedy or crisis for that matter) from reaching out. Instead, ask, "How can I help you?" and follow up with action.

✔ Make sure a divorcee has a place to go during times when other families may be gathering. Invite him or her (and children if applicable) to family dinners, game nights, movies, etc. Chances are, a divorcee will say no, feeling they are an inconvenience. The vicious thought of, "My former spouse didn't want me, so why would you?" circulates in their minds. Make the invitation sincere, and don't give up if they say no the first time. Accept their offer to bring something to contribute for dinner.

✔ Send a card. Only don't just send a card, but take time to personalize it with an encouraging note that affirms its recipient. Also consider dropping in some cash or a gift card, as well. Even $5 for a coffee or smoothie is a luxury some folks can't afford.

✔ Ask when a good time might be to bring by a casserole or drop off a gift card for dinner. Self-care is often one of the last things a divorcee has time for. Making sure your fellow church members eat good meals is a necessity.

✔ Are kids involved? Offer to babysit. Give the mom or dad a Friday night off so he or she can have a night with friends or simply go grocery shopping alone. Divorced individuals who shoulder the brunt of custody agreements sometimes find socialization a struggle.

✔ In the absence of a male around, some women may need help hanging blinds or curtain rods In a new house. If you're a master with a power drill, offer to stop by for some maintenance. In the absence of a female around, some men may not yet have the skills to adequately clean, do laundry, cook, or mend. Consider offering to fill a void that might otherwise have been filled.

✔ Invite him or her to participate fully in the life of the church. Many who are divorced do pull back from extra responsibilities outside of family and work following a separation for mental, physical and emotional reasons — and that can be a good thing. However, spiritually, a divorce can create feelings of doubt and unworthiness about qualifications for leadership and service. Never allow a change in marital status to impede someone's desire to serve within your congregation.

(ideas taken from a previously distributed blog post by the author)

Side Dish: Physical & Mental Illness

Love Feast 31

Physical and Mental Illness

Illness is another area in which the church has often had much introduction into Pastoral Care. It is typical for pastors, priests, and congregations to go visit those who are sick and homebound — those who have illnesses that are visible and recognizable.

However, the church has not done a very good job at responding to individuals with mental illness, illnesses that are not visible, or carry a stigma such as depression, anxiety, chronic fatigue, fibromyalgia, addiction, HIV/AIDS, etc.

Physical Illness — Pastoral Care can be offered to individuals who experience short-term physical illness such as a broken bone, influenza, pneumonia, etc., and it can be offered to individuals experiencing long-term illnesses such as cancer, heart failure, organ failure, dementia, etc., that may or may not come with hospitalizations or stays in assisted living facilities.

What other ways can physical illnesses be more visible than a mental illness?

Mental illness symptoms often manifest themselves physically, as well, through headaches, chronic fatigue, chronic pain, and troubles sleeping or staying awake. These symptoms, however, are still "invisible" to those outside an individual's inner circle.

Brainstorm reasons why the Church has been hesitant to minister actively to those with mental illness. How might the Church transform its responses to those with mental, or "invisible," illnesses?

Side Dish: Physical & Mental Illness

What is depression?

Everyone feels depressed or down at some point. If some or all of these symptoms are experienced most of the day, nearly every day, for two weeks or more, an individual may be experiencing <u>clinical depression</u> and need to seek help and care:

- ✔ persistent sad, anxious or "empty" mood
- ✔ feelings of hopelessness or pessimism
- ✔ irritability
- ✔ feelings of guilt, worthlessness or helplessness
- ✔ loss of interest in things that formerly brought pleasure
- ✔ decreased energy or fatigue
- ✔ moving or talking more slowly
- ✔ feeling restless
- ✔ difficulty concentrating
- ✔ difficulty sleeping or staying awake
- ✔ appetite and/or weight changes
- ✔ thoughts of death or suicide
- ✔ aches, pains, headaches, cramps, digestive problems without a clear cause that do not go away easily with or without treatment

(https://www.nimh.nih.gov/health/topics/depression/index.shtml)

Depression can be caused by changes in brain chemicals, illness, major life changes including loss and grief, substance abuse, certain medications, and family history. Short-term depression can be expected and can go away with time and healing. Long-term depression often needs to be treated with counseling and medication.

(What everyone should know about depression - Channing Bete Company 2012)

What NOT to say to those experiencing depression:

- ✘ If you just prayed more, you'd feel better.
- ✘ Give it to God; God will heal it in God's time.
- ✘ Cheer up!
- ✘ Think positively!

Side Dish: Physical & Mental Illness

Love Feast 33

Suicide

Annually, there are an estimated 25,000 suicides. Suicide has been called, controversially, weakness, a noble act, a sin, a crime, a disease, a natural choice.
(Asquith 217)

While we may not be able to agree on the theology that surrounds suicide, what we can all agree on is that it is a tragedy worth preventing when possible, and properly grieving when not.

Pastoral Understanding of Suicide:

1. Depression and isolation — most suicidal persons are lonely, depressed individuals experiencing strong feelings of hopelessness and helplessness, and perhaps anger, and often have tried various ways to find a solution to their emotional distress.

2. Ambivalence — the desires for life and death are in conflict. Most are not necessarily wanting to die as they are willing to die as a necessary price to escape the seemingly endless pain.

3. Crisis — most suicidal persons will make a serious attempt during a relatively brief emotional crisis. Clinical experience shows that if a suicidal person survives the crisis due to outside intervention, the individual doesn't return quickly to the high-risk stage

4. Communication — individuals contemplating suicide often make overt and covert attempts at communicating their pain and thoughts.

Pastoral Intervention of Suicide:

1. Listening — most suicidal people respond well when distress and depression are received by a sensitive, concerned listener.

2. Evaluating suicidal risk — Those who are seriously considering suicide often have a concrete plan and have contemplated how to carry out their death. The more specific and detailed the plan and means, the higher the risk will be.

3. Intervention plan — an intervention plan should focus on the immediate issues and be implemented quickly, even if it only offers a temporary solution. A list of all existing resources should be developed, and the suicidal person should participate fully in creating a plan. Follow up is important for those intervening.

4. Referral — In all high-risk situations, and those in which there is doubt, professional consultation should be sought.
(Asquith 218-220)

Side Dish: Addiction

Addiction

Addiction comes with so many societal stigmas it can be hard to correctly identify and minister to as it is often hidden from the general public for fear of judgment, retaliation, punishment, etc. Christians can all work together to take away the stigma of addiction and work to heal the God-sized hole in everyone's hearts — addicted or not.

Addicted to what?

- ✔ Drugs (cocaine, heroin, prescription drugs, marijuana)
- ✔ Alcohol
- ✔ Sex
- ✔ Pornography
- ✔ Gambling
- ✔ Food
- ✔ Power
- ✔ Worry
- ✔ Money
- ✔ Work

Anything "healthy" in excess can become an addiction when it usurps God's place as No. 1 priority in our lives. Most doctrine would label that priority valuation as "idolatry."

"Alcoholics just have their powerlessness visible for all to see. The rest of us disguise it in different ways, and overcompensate for our more hidden and subtle addictions and attachments, especially our addiction to our way of thinking."

(Richard Rohr, Breathing Under Water, xviii)

Causes of Addiction:
- ■ Hereditary
- ■ Genetics and environmental factors
- ■ Using and abusing addictive substances before the brain is fully developed may increase risk of later addiction

(https://americanaddictioncenters.org/rehab-guide/addiction-statistics/)

Side Dish: Addiction

For many addicts, an outside force **CANNOT** diagnose addiction. Addiction must be self-diagnosed and self-admitted before pursuing healing, treatment and care with much success. This is the primary first step in the Twelve Steps of Alcoholics Anonymous, which is not just for alcoholics: "We admitted we were powerless over alcohol — that our lives had become unmanageable."

(*Twelve Steps and Twelve Traditions*, Bill Wilson)

Monologue vs. Dialogue

Addicts live in a world that focuses on self. They are imprisoned in an "iron bubble."

Chooses:
- ✔ Non-relatedness
- ✔ Self-centeredness
- ✔ Isolation

God speaking through others cannot breach the prison

God of his or her understanding has no point of entry

Individual in Recovery begin to live in a world that includes others and experience liberation.

Chooses:
- ✔ Relatedness
- ✔ Love
- ✔ Trust
- ✔ Gratitude
- ✔ Honesty

Can hear the voice of God through many platforms

God of his or her understanding has many points of entry, especially other people

(*The Essence of Twelve Step Recovery*, Damian McElrath, 8-9)

Is there a **cure for addiction**? Most addicts will say no. Every day is a struggle, some more than others. But each day is an opportunity to experience God's grace, and the renewal of commitment to keep healing.

Discuss if your church is ready to minister to an individual who may never be "cured" of what ails him or her. Why or why not?

Side Dish: Addiction

Enabling vs. Empowering

It is natural to want to help someone who isn't in a position to help themselves. But a trap many fall into when helping those with addiction, especially close friends and family members, is the habit of enabling that individual to continue in their way of addiction.

Signs of enabling

1. Denial — refusing to accept the reality that the loved one is an addict

2. Justification — rejecting the true nature of the problem to find a more worthy "cause" of abuse

3. Allowing substance abuse — allowing that abuse to occur at home in an effort to control the behavior

4. Suppressing feelings — honest expression of feelings, even of anger, resentment and fear, can be healthy for an addict to hear

5. Protecting the family's image — portraying that person in a positive light to others so the stigma of addiction doesn't permeate the home

6. Minimizing the situation or avoiding the problem — addiction is not a phase that will go away on its own

7. Playing the blame game — punishing or blaming individuals for their addiction can potentially alienate them even further from those they love

8. Assuming responsibilities — taking over an addict's tasks and responsibilities, and giving them money in order to prevent their life from falling apart allows that individual to fully indulge in their addiction

9. Controlling behaviors — constantly treating the addict as inferior or restricting their lifestyle may drive them closer to the addiction

Actions of **empowerment** may include letting that individual fail in personal responsibilities. Empowerment can also be displayed by paying for rehabilitation services when that individual is ready, attending counseling sessions with the individual, or attending counseling sessions yourself in order to be a better support of that loved one.

(https://www.drugrehab.com/addiction/enabling-vs-helping/)

Side Dish: Addiction

The Twelve Steps of Alcoholics Anonymous

1. We admitted we were powerless over alcohol — that our lives had become unmanageable.
2. Came to believe that a Power greater than ourselves could restore us to sanity.
3. Made a decision to turn our will and our lives over to the care of God as we understood Him.
4. Made a searching and fearless moral inventory of ourselves.
5. Admitted to God, to ourselves, and to another human being the exact nature of our wrongs.
6. Were entirely ready to have God remove all these defects of character.
7. Humbly asked Him to remove our shortcomings.
8. Made a list of all persons we had harmed, and became willing to make amends to them all.
9. Made direct amends to such people wherever possible, except when to do so would injure them or others.
10. Continued to take personal inventory and when we were wrong promptly admitted it.
11. Sought through prayer and meditation to improve our conscious contact with God as we understood Him, praying only for knowledge of His will for us and the power to carry that out.
12. Having had a spiritual awakening as the result of these steps, we tried to carry this message to alcoholics, and to practice these principles in all our affairs.

Additional Programs:
For more information on recovery programs, visit http://www.celebraterecovery.com. Celebrate Recovery is a program started at Rev. Rick Warren's Saddleback Church in California where participants can work on their "hurts, habits and hang-ups."

Side Dish: Veterans & PTSD

Veterans and PTSD

The new millennia has ushered in a new time of war and conflict that has required U.S. military intervention. Many individuals have served time in the military, and are coming home in greater numbers due to advances in technology and medicine, whereas in past wars and conflicts, individuals sadly might not have come home at all.

Who is a veteran?
The term veteran includes ALL who have served in the military, not just those who have experienced war or military conflict.

Struggles for veterans returning home after prolonged absences:
- Unemployment
- Marriage/family issues
- Self-esteem or identity issues
- Physical issues, such as loss of limb or function
- Post-traumatic stress disorder (PTSD)
- Substance abuse
- Depression

Spiritual Struggles and Issues — after seeing and experiencing some of the atrocities of war, it is logical that spirituality may suffer for a veteran upon returning home. Veterans may experience:

- Guilt for things he or she did, and for things they didn't do
- Survivor's guilt
- "Lost my faith/lost my soul overseas"
- Growth of faith
- Questions of God and theodicy
- Loss of trust in God or others
- Loss of community and relationships
- Moral injury — perpetrating, failing to prevent, doing something or learning about something that transgresses who you are and moral norms (could be a betrayal by a leader in enticing the individual into unethical action)

(Chaplain Steve Sullivan, VA/Clergy Partnership for Rural Veterans)

Side Dish: Veterans & PTSD

What is PTSD?
Post-traumatic stress disorder is a mental health condition that occurs after an individual experiences directly or indirectly a traumatic, life-altering event such as combat, natural disaster, rape, abuse, car accident, etc.

Veterans experiencing PTSD
- 30 percent of Vietnam veterans
- 10 percent of Gulf War veterans
- 11 percent of Afghanistan war veterans
- 20 percent of Iraqi war veterans

(https://www.ptsd.va.gov/public/PTSD-overview/basics/how-common-is-ptsd.asp)

What are the symptoms of PTSD?
1. Reliving the event through flashbacks, memories or nightmares
2. Avoiding situations that remind you of the event
3. Having more negative beliefs and feelings - depression, guilt, shame, feeling the world is dangerous, numbness
4. Hyperarousal — jittery, always on alert or on the lookout for danger, trouble concentrating or sleeping

(https://www.ptsd.va.gov/public/PTSD-overview/basics/what-is-ptsd.asp)

How can we help?
- ✔ Suspend judgment; be willing to sit with moral ambiguity
- ✔ Don't ask if he or she killed anyone
- ✔ Offer them grace and forgiveness judiciously
- ✔ Accept them where they are, not where they used to be or where they should be
- ✔ Pay attention: books, links, movies, NPR — can open doors to conversation and understanding

(Chaplain Steve Sullivan, VA/Clergy Partnership for Rural Veterans)

Side Dish: Veterans & PTSD

How faith communities can help veterans and families readjust

Families filled voids left by the soldier, and new roles were assumed with new rules. While the soldier's family is the same, it is a newer model. The soldier's role in the family may have changed. Family, friends, and coworkers may have "leapt ahead" while the soldier was "frozen in time" and is left to try and sync with a new world.

The soldier returns from a life of danger to a life of uncertainty. In combat training, the solider mastered dependence on peers, vigilance, reactive obedience, and weaponry. The military directed and provided. Back as a civilian, the soldier must live by complex societal codes and often resume the role as provider. In combat, the soldier felt safe within the confines of the base and his or her team. At home, the soldier, now unarmed and away from his or her team, may feel vulnerable and not sure where or if he or she is safe and secure.

Faith communities have a unique opportunity to help veterans and their families. Consider these steps to ministering to veterans around you:

1. <u>Make your community "military friendly"</u> — You don't have to be on the same page regarding US foreign policy or promote war, but you can still respect, honor, serve and care for veterans and their families affected by those things.

2. <u>Reach out to military families</u> — walk with them through the separation or reunion

3. <u>Reach out to the deployed soldier</u> — letters and care packages are great

4. <u>Welcome the solider home</u> — if public, make sure you do this with consent

5. <u>Support beyond the homecoming</u> — don't overwhelm the family, but don't ignore their situation, either

6. <u>Listen, support, absolve</u> — without condemning

7. <u>Be alert for signs of distress</u> — showing up for worship doesn't always mean everything is healthy at home

(adapted by VA chaplain David Lundell from www.speakingoffaith.org - The Soul of War)

Dessert: Worship

Dessert - Worship

If your engagement with this curriculum includes more than one person, worship together! Use this order of worship as a springboard for praising God for allowing us to be a part of Jesus Christ's caring ministry on Earth.

Call to Worship

Leader: The Lord is my Shepherd
Group: May we love others like Jesus Christ

Leader: He leads me beside still waters; he restores my soul
Group: May we serve others in a selfless fashion

Leader: Even though I walk through the valley of the shadow of death
Group: May we fear no evil as we comfort others

Leader: You prepare a table before me in the presence of my enemies
Group: May the Carpenter build us a bigger table

All: May we share with others the green pastures and calm lands that God has given us. May we share the fruits of our labor, and may we minister alongside each other as servants. Amen.

Open with Prayer

Old Testament Scripture Reading
Ecclesiastes 3:1-8, ESV

3 For everything there is a season, and a time for every matter under heaven:
2 a time to be born, and a time to die;
a time to plant, and a time to pluck up what is planted;
3 a time to kill, and a time to heal;
a time to break down, and a time to build up;
4 a time to weep, and a time to laugh;
a time to mourn, and a time to dance;

Dessert: Worship

5 a time to cast away stones, and a time to gather stones together;
a time to embrace, and a time to refrain from embracing;
6 a time to seek, and a time to lose;
a time to keep, and a time to cast away;
7 a time to tear, and a time to sew;
a time to keep silence, and a time to speak;
8 a time to love, and a time to hate;
a time for war, and a time for peace.

Song: The Servant Song by Richard Gillard

Neighbor, let me be your servant.
Let me be as Christ to you.
Pray that I might have the grace
To let you be my servant, too.

We are pilgrims on a journey.
We are brothers on the road.
We are here to help each other
Walk the mile and bear the load.

I will hold the Christ-light for you
In the night time of your fear.
I will hold my hand out to you;
Speak the peace you long to hear.

I will weep when you are weeping.
When you laugh, I'll laugh with you.
I will share your joy and sorrow
Till we've seen this journey through.

When we sing to God in heaven,
We shall find such harmony
Born of all we've known together
Of Christ's love and agony.

Other song choices could include: Lifesong by Casting Crowns or Here I am, Lord, by Dan Schutte

Dessert: Worship

Prayers of the People
Take this time to share the names and situations of those who need to feel Christ's care, compassion and love in your homes, your congregation and your community.

New Testament Scripture Reading:
Romans 15:1-7 NRSV

"We who are strong ought to put up with the failings of the weak, and not to please ourselves. 2 Each of us must please our neighbor for the good purpose of building up the neighbor. 3 For Christ did not please himself; but, as it is written, 'The insults of those who insult you have fallen on me.' 4 For whatever was written in former days was written for our instruction, so that by steadfastness and by the encouragement of the scriptures we might have hope. 5 May the God of steadfastness and encouragement grant you to live in harmony with one another, in accordance with Christ Jesus, 6 so that together you may with one voice glorify the God and Father of our Lord Jesus Christ.
7 Welcome one another, therefore, just as Christ has welcomed you, for the glory of God."

Holy Communion
Serve communion as your tradition dictates.

Close with this prayer, read together:

Healer, Sustainer, Reconciler, Our Shining Guide, Almighty God — we are grateful for your mercy and grace. We thank you for your Holy Spirit, the Helper who is alive and working in us and through the world. We thank you for each other. We ask that you show us how to love others, how to care for others, how to heal others, how to walk with others as Christ has done all of those things for each of us. Forgive us when we ignore those who are hungry, when we turn away those who are thirsty, when we rebuke those who are in need. Let us welcome others as you first welcomed us. In your humble son Jesus' name we pray — Amen.

Personal Reflection

Personal Reflection

Every good meal has a moment of quiet reflection, a time where the feast has nourished, the conversation was meaningful, and memories were made. Use these prompts to help you digest some of the items and issues talked about in this curriculum. Write your thoughts in a personal journal.

Personal Reflection 1

Create a list, writing down your best qualities. On a separate list, write down the qualities that might make it hard for someone to love you. Write a prayer thanking God for loving you anyway, asking God to show you how to love and show Christ-like care to others no matter the circumstances.

Personal Reflection 2

Who in your congregation needs Pastoral Care? Make a list of individuals, families or groups who need to see an example of Christ's love and care. Of that list, pick out at least three to care for in the coming month, and create a plan to put your thoughts into action.

Personal Reflection 3

Recall a time where you received Pastoral Care. What about that action ministered to you? Write a letter thanking that individual, congregation or group for their ministry, pointing out specific things that were done to make you feel the love and care of Christ. Share it with that party.

Personal Reflection 4

Recall a time where you were not given adequate Pastoral Care. What could have been done to properly minister to you at that time in your life? How might you have helped others minister to you, or sought out others' help, in that circumstance? Write a prayer of forgiveness for those who were not able, willing, or knowledgeable enough to act out the love and care of Christ.

Bibliography

Sources

Books

Asquith Jr., Glenn H. <u>The Concise Dictionary of Pastoral Care and Counseling</u>. Abingdon Press, 2010.

McElrath, Damian. <u>The Essence of Twelve Step Recovery: Take It to Heart</u>. Hazelden, 2008.

Rohr, Richard. <u>Breathing Under Water: Spirituality and the Twelve Steps</u>. Franciscan Media, 2011.

<u>What everyone should know about depression</u>. Channing Bete Company, 2012.

Wilson, Bill. <u>Twelve Steps and Twelve Traditions</u>. Alcoholics Anonymous World Services, Inc., 2001.

Websites

American Addiction Centers
https://americanaddictioncenters.org/rehab-guide/addiction-statistics/

American Psychology Association
http://www.apa.org/topics/divorce/

Centers for Disease Control
https://www.cdc.gov/nchs/fastats/marriage-divorce.htm

Drug Rehab
https://www.drugrehab.com/addiction/enabling-vs-helping/

National Institute for Mental Health
https://www.nimh.nih.gov/health/topics/depression/index.shtml

Psychology Today
https://www.psychologytoday.com/blog/living-single/201702/what-is-the-divorce-rate-really

U.S. Department of Veterans Affairs - National Center for PTSD
https://www.ptsd.va.gov/public/PTSD-overview/basics/how-common-is-ptsd.asp
https://www.ptsd.va.gov/public/PTSD-overview/basics/what-is-ptsd.asp

Articles

"How faith communities can help veterans and their families readjust" - adapted by VA chaplain David Lundell from www.speakingoffaith.org - The Soul of War

Lectures

Introduction to the Theology and Practice of Pastoral Care class at Memphis Theological Seminary, Fall 2017 - taught by Dr. Lee Ramsey

Presentation by Chaplain Steve Sullivan, VA/Clergy Partnership for Rural Veterans